Dubai

A PICTORIAL SOUVENIR

D1306293

Published with the support
and encouragement of

DUBAI DUTY FREE

Dubai

A PICTORIAL SOUVENIR

MOTIVATE
PUBLISHING

Published by
Motivate Publishing

Dubai: PO Box 2331, Dubai, UAE
Tel: (+971 4) 282 4060, fax (+971 4) 282 0428
e-mail: books@motivate.co.ae   www.booksarabia.com

Abu Dhabi: PO Box 43072, Abu Dhabi, UAE
Tel: (+971 2) 627 1666, fax (+971 2) 627 1566

London: 4 Middle Street, London EC1A 7NQ
e-mail: motivateuk@motivate.co.ae

Directors:
Obaid Humaid Al Tayer and Ian Fairservice

Written and edited by:
Jackie Nel and David Steele

Editorial and photographic research:
Alison Ashbee, Catherine Demangeot and Zelda Pinto

Designer: Johnson Machado

© **Motivate Publishing 2001**

First published 2001
Reprinted 2002

Printed by:
Rashid Printers & Stationers LLC, Ajman, UAE

ISBN: 1 86063 056 1

British Library Cataloguing-in-Publication Data. A catalogue record for this book
is available from the British Library.

Cover: Camels, an essential part of life in the desert, are still very much a feature of the Dubai landscape.
Title page: Jumeirah Mosque is one of the city's landmarks.
This page: Dubai is blessed with year-round warm, sunny weather and several beautiful beaches on which to make the most of it.

Introduction

from His Highness Sheikh Hamdan bin Rashid Al Maktoum, Deputy Ruler of Dubai, UAE Minister of Finance and Industry, and Chairman of Dubai Municipality

If you are new to Dubai, welcome – and I hope this book will serve as a useful introduction. For residents or visitors already familiar with the emirate, I believe it will present some perspectives of our country and history you may not have seen before.

For those who have recently arrived I suggest that, to get a feel for the place and to begin to understand how it works, you take a stroll along the Creek. Appropriately, the waterway features dominantly in this book, simply because it's been so dominant in our history. The activities there are a microcosm of the whole of this industrious, multicultural, adaptable, tolerant city.

The Creek curves through Dubai, its waters reflecting ancient wind-towers and neon advertisements, its skyline alternately punctuated by slender minarets and high-rise offices. Moored at its wharfs or churning its surface are trading dhows and fishing boats, pleasure craft and oil-service vessels. Hotels and gardens line its banks, while the walls of the merchants' houses in the old quarter are still lapped by its tides. Busy along its shores are the people of many nations who live and work here, bringing a cultural variety that enriches every aspect of life.

Geography, of course, has helped. Dubai, positioned midway between Europe and the Far Fast, is at the hub of the wealthy Middle East and of a greater market that stretches from the Levant to the Indian subcontinent and from the newly-emerging states of the CIS to Africa. But then, throughout the world, strategic locations, especially seaports, have historically been centres of trading activity – although not all have taken full advantage of their position by developing trading skills and supporting services, nor have they all attracted commerce and industry.

Here in Dubai – while we have the necessary controls and legislation to secure a fair and just commercial environment – the authorities prefer to leave companies to get on with what they do best: running their businesses.

The success of this policy can be evidenced by a few statistics. In 1958 Dubai's imports totalled some $6 million; in 1988 $6,243 million; in 2000 $19,346 million. Dubai has always been ready to trade, and to invest in an infrastructure that's already attracted so much commerce and industry to the emirate – ports and cargo facilities, accommodation and telecommunications, modern road systems and an award-winning airline.

In addition to the benefits offered by the city itself, the Free Zones at Jebel Ali (which has been chosen by more than 1,500 companies as their Gulf base) and at Dubai Media City, Dubai Internet City and Dubai International Airport have been designed to provide a congenial business environment. The people who live and work here are catered for by a host of ancillary services ranging from education to entertainment, sports and leisure facilities, hospitals and clinics, high-quality housing and ease of access for travellers and goods.

While Dubai's history can be traced back some 6,000 years, there has probably been more change in the last three decades than in the preceding six millennia. Even as recently as the early 1950s Dubai was still a small entrepôt trading port, the occupants of which, since the decline of the pearl trade a generation earlier, had returned to earning a modest living from the import and re-export of goods.

Then, the regular P&O steamships from Bombay would anchor a mile offshore, their cargoes and passengers being brought to land by small boats of sufficiently shallow draught to enter the creek. At the desert airstrip, the occasional DC3, Heron and Dove would whisk up the sand on the unpaved runways. Few people could anticipate the immense changes that would take place in the years ahead.

But one man could. His Highness Sheikh Rashid bin Saeed Al Maktoum, whose son Sheikh Maktoum so ably continues our late father's policies, combined the shrewdness and trading skills of a merchant with the foresight of a visionary. If you would like to see his monument, stand at any vantage point in Dubai and look around – not just at the buildings themselves, impressive as they are, but also at the people, the activity and the way of life: together, they form a unique and still-developing testament.

Hamdan bin Rashid Al Maktoum

Along the Creek

a head – a great experience for independent-minded visitors. The *abras* provide a leisurely, old-fashioned way to journey about in the very heart of a fast-paced, modern commercial centre. Larger pleasure boats offering dinner cruises with a view are also on hand.

There's plenty to do along the Creek banks too. Near the Creek mouth, in the Shindagha district, a heritage village and the replica of an old pearl-diving village provide fascinating insights into Dubai's traditional culture. Also in Shindagha, former ruler Sheikh Saeed Al Maktoum's sandstone home has now become a museum, with its traditional wind-towers (old-fashioned air-conditioning) and displays of historical photographs and mementoes.

Further up is the Cloth Souk. With its blaze of colourful raw silks and cottons hanging in profusion from the many shop windows, it captures the atmosphere of the souks of a bygone era wonderfully. At the beginning of the souk is Bur Dubai's main *abra* stand.

Just outside the souk is the Ruler's Diwan, or government office. Then comes the historical Bastakiya district with its narrow lanes and tall wind-towers, giving another tantalising glimpse of the Dubai of yesteryear. The district is currently undergoing renovation and preservation.

A scenic stroll along the promenade here can be particularly beautiful at sunset, when you'll see golden reflections of the water and dhows in the high-rise buildings that line the Creek; the striking National Bank

Dubai is a city divided by a waterway, a salt-water inlet known as the Creek. The Creek is the reason for Dubai's existence – the first settlement was established on its banks – and it's still the main artery of Dubai, separating Bur Dubai on one side from Deira on the other. A stroll along its banks evokes the city's centuries-old trading traditions and the colour and bustle of the loading and unloading of dhows, which still ply ancient trade routes to India and Africa, easily captivates the imagination.

The best way to see the Creek is from the water, and picturesque water-taxis known as *abras* putter back and forth cross the Creek at a very affordable half-a-dirham of Dubai building, with its curved façade of polished steel and glass, was in fact custom-designed for this purpose.

The ultra-modern architecture of this building, as well as the other glass and concrete towers nearby, such as Twin Towers and the eye-catching Chamber of Commerce and Industry, stand in intriguing juxtaposition to the dhows below. However, there's a pleasing sense of continuity in the commercial buildings having the trading dhows at their feet.

There are two bridges over the Creek: Al Maktoum Bridge and Al Garhoud Bridge. Between them, on the Bur Dubai side, is Creek Park, a popular recreational area with its cableway, barbecue sites and acres of landscaped gardens. Beyond Garhoud Bridge the upper reaches of the Creek are used for water sports such as rowing and jet-skiing.

At the top, inland, end of the Creek is a shallow lagoon which has been turned into a bird sanctuary; flamingos are the most conspicuous but there are vast numbers of other birds, particularly during the migration, when up to 27,000 birds have been counted at a time.

Returning along the Creek on the Deira side, the first noteworthy sight is the huge development just before Al Garhoud Bridge: Dubai Festival City. It will be a waterfront destination that stretches for all of four kilometres, with a marina, restaurants, shops, entertainment facilities (including an amphitheatre), hotels and offices.

Across the bridge is the Dubai Creek Golf and Yacht Club – the clubhouse, resembling a dhow under full sail, is a landmark in itself. The complex incorporates a 115-berth marina and, besides the world-class sporting facilities, it houses several interesting restaurants from which to enjoy the glamorous views (and where the public are welcome).

Across the next (Al Maktoum) bridge is the dhow wharfage. Today, the dhows use engines rather than sails, but are still traditional in shape; this is a fascinating area to explore with a camera and extends past a waterfront development with upmarket hotels and luxury cabin cruisers to the *abra* station.

This marks the gateway to the souks of Deira, where you'll find a maze of narrow alleyways and tiny, very affordable pavement café-style eateries, as well as the atmospheric, crowded-with-merchandise little shops so typical of Dubai.

The Creek (and the road that borders it) makes a sharp U-turn before it flows into the Gulf, creating a finger of land which projects into the water. In this area you'll find the famous Gold Souk and nearer the mouth (close to where the Shindagha Tunnel passes under the Creek) the Deira fish, meat and vegetable market – which also marks the end of the round trip.

Previous spread: A leisurely boat trip along the Creek will reveal, along with many of the economic and architectural landmarks of the emirate, the true spirit of Dubai.

The existence of a Creek was the reason for a settlement becoming established here in the early days of Arab seafaring. Today, the Creek remains at the heart of Dubai's development as well as its economic life, while still giving the city a unique cachet.

While dhows are now propelled by engines rather than the lateen sails of yesteryear, they are still built in the traditional way, by craftsmen whose expertise renders the use of blueprints unnecessary.

The Creek is the centre of Dubai's re-export activities. These dhows, moored three and four abreast, still ply trading routes to India, Pakistan, East Asia and within the Gulf, re-distributing goods throughout the region.

*On a stroll along the northern bank of the Creek, the
loading and unloading of a variety of cargo, which might
even include a car or pick-up vehicle, can be witnessed.*

The heart of the city is where traditional vessels coexist with some of the most modern architecture, such as the Twin Towers (left), which houses luxury apartments with a panoramic view, offices and a shopping mall.

The curved glass façade of the National Bank of Dubai building provides breathtaking reflections of the Creek. These vary throughout the day, but are at their most dramatic at sunset.

Aptly sited near the dhow wharf, the Dubai Chamber of Commerce and Industry has overseen the economic transformation of Dubai from a centre of traditional trade to one of the main economic poles east of the European continent.

Rising side by side, the buildings of the Dubai Chamber of Commerce and Industry and the National Bank of Dubai seem to be engaged in a keen architectural duel.

A glass façade alongside the Creek shows the Emirates Towers building in the background, as well as the greenery of the promenade on the southern bank of the Creek.

Abras *provide constant traffic on the Creek, and many people use them as their main means of transportation.*

Dubai is really made up of two main areas – Bur Dubai and Deira. These abras, or water taxis, wait to transport passengers from one bank of the Creek to the other in just a few minutes – and for a mere Dhs 0.50 a trip.

In addition to their usual ferry duties, abras can be rented by the hour for longer sight-seeing journeys down the Creek.

Opposite page: The Ruler's Diwan, or government office, on the southern bank of the Creek occupies a traditional building adorned with wind-towers.

A view of the Creek from the pleasant southern bank promenade – a delightful place from which to watch the sunset reflections.

23

Inspired by tradition

*T*he Dubai we see today is built on foundations which are rich in history and tradition: the Arabian heritage is still proudly recognised and the ancient customs are still practised in everyday life. Most notably, many nationals still wear traditional dress, which is adapted to religious beliefs and high temperatures. The men wear a *kandoura* (an ankle-length, loose-fitting white shirt-dress) and *gutra* (a cotton headcloth) held in place by an *igal* (woollen headrope), while women wear an *abaya* (a long-sleeved, full-length black dress). The hair is covered with a *shayla* (scarf) and the face may also be covered by a *gishwa* (thin veil). Some women wear a *burqa* (stiff material face masks to cover the eyebrows, nose and mouth) instead of a veil.

Traditional festivals are also strictly observed, the key one being Ramadan, the Holy Month in which Muslims commemorate the revelation of the Qur'an. It's a month (the timing depends on the moon) of fasting from dawn to dusk, when Muslims – and often, out of respect, those who work or mix with them – refrain from eating, drinking, smoking or chewing gum.

Iftar is the sunset time when people can start eating again; at this time of day, it's not unusual to find taxis pulled over on the side of the road and the drivers tucking into an Iftar snack. Eid Al Fitr is a feast which marks the end of the month of Ramadan and lasts for three or four days. The *shisha* or hubble-bubble (water) pipe is conspicuous among these Iftar celebrations – and indeed throughout the year. It's usually savoured in a café or restaurant while chatting to friends; if you walk past any pavement café you'll smell the distinctive fruit-flavoured tobacco, usually apple.

The rich Arabian heritage is further celebrated in a number of tourist sites, Heritage Village being just one appropriately-named example. This village showcases the arts, crafts, traditions and lifestyles of the region – it includes a replica of a pearl-diving village, once the primary source of income – and aims to take the visitor back in time to the Dubai of yesteryear.

Sheikh Saeed Al Maktoum's House, also in Shindagha, dates to the late 1800s and was built near the mouth of the Creek so the then ruler could watch the shipping activity from the balconies. Today, it's been turned into a museum. With its wind-towers and central courtyard, it's a fine example of traditional achitecture.

The Dubai Museum housed in Al Fahidi Fort, in itself a fascinating destination for military buffs, has intriguing dioramas, complete with life-size figures and sound and lighting effects, to depict everyday life in pre-oil days. Galleries recreate traditional scenes from the Creek, Arab houses, mosques, souks, deserts and pearl-diving.

Jumeirah Mosque is another prime example of traditional Islamic architecture. Arguably Dubai's most beautiful mosque, and built of stone, it's particularly attractive at night when the subtle lighting throws its artistic twin minarets and majestic dome into relief. In a bid to promote understanding, the mosque has now opened it doors to guided tours for visitors. Here they can ask questions about Islam and learn more about Arabian heritage.

From mosques to souks, the Arabian markets: the goods on offer may have expanded from spices and silks to include electronic goods and ready-made garments, but the atmosphere of a bustling market place with all its accompanying noisy bargaining remains. The Gold Souk in Deira is probably the most visited, but the Covered Souk and the Spice Souk should not be missed.

As much a part of Arab heritage as souks are camels, and on any longish journey out of town you'll see them wandering alongside – and sometimes on – the road. Once the most cherished possession of the nomadic Bedu tribes, camels are still highly prized animals. One of the best ways to see them is at the camel races on the outskirts of the city.

The Arabian horse, of course, is another treasured animal and horse-racing, whether on the track or in the desert in the form of endurance racing is another very popular pastime. The involvement of several sheikhs ensures high-profile publicity and a great deal of financial sport.

Falconry is another popular – and traditional – pastime. The birds are extremely highly valued by their owners and the close relationship between the two is the key to success. Falconry displays are most commonly seen at tourist destinations such as the Heritage Village but, if you do venture a little off the beaten track, you may be lucky enough to see the real thing.

Previous spread: The imposing compound of Sheikh Saeed's House stands in Shindagha, between the Creek and the sea. It was the residence of the ruling Al Maktoum family until 1958.

27

The Heritage Village is a great place to sample traditional Arabic food – such as flat bread.

Climbing up the well head: Such structures, seen in the towns and the desert, are used to draw water from an underground well.

The Heritage Village in Shindagha is the place to visit for an insight into the traditional lifestyle of the region: This campsite gathering recalls the nomadic past of the Bedu.

Until 40 years ago, many of the houses were made of palm fronds: The interstices in the façade would let the air circulate and provide some relief from the heat.

Sheikh Saeed's House in Shindagha was built to take full advantage of the breeze from the sea and the Creek. On its wide terraces and in the large, airy rooms with their many windows, even the fierce heat of summer seems a little abated.

The house is now a museum containing artefacts such as model craft,
stamps, coins, documents and weapons, as well as evocative photographs,
which enable the visitor to appreciate the origins and recent past of the city.

Dubai Museum's most memorable exhibit is the underground gallery through which visitors meander past life-like dioramas and multimedia presentations providing a fascinating insight into Dubai's past.

Al Fahidi Fort, built around the middle of the 19th century, was used to protect the people of Dubai from tribal conflict. In later periods, it was successively the seat of government, an arms-and-ammunition store, and the central jail. It now houses Dubai Museum.

Houses were typically built round a central courtyard, with every room opening onto it. This fine example houses one of Dubai's oldest art galleries.

Left: The wind-tower, essentially an early form of air-conditioning, was brought to Dubai by Iranians who settled in Bastakiya in the early 20th century. The square towers are divided diagonally to form four triangular shafts. Any passing breeze causes air to be pushed down the tower and sucked up again, generating a welcome draught below.

Below: Bastakiya, the former merchant area on the south side of the Creek, has the distinctive traditional architecture of imposing houses with wind-towers; many of these have been carefully restored.

The deep faith of the Muslims is embodied in omnipresent mosques, the largest of which is the Jumeirah Mosque. Tours of the inside of this mosque are organised by the Sheikh Mohammed Centre for Cultural Understanding.

While the lifestyle in Dubai is among the most modern in the world, the traditions of Arabia are still practised in everyday life, particularly during family and religious occasions. This dance, where women swirl their long hair with graceful movements of their heads, is often performed at weddings and public celebrations.

In Arab culture, a favourite way to relax is to celebrate a wedding or special occasion – and music is always an integral part of the event.

Left: The Gold Souk has to be one of the most impressive sights for visitors, with shop window after shop window displaying miles of glittering gold jewellery. Dubai is said to be one of the cheapest places in the world to buy gold.

Above: Trade, the source of Dubai's economic strength, is vividly highlighted as you wander along the souks. In this souk, textiles can be bought in retail or wholesale quantities.

Left: The souks are a wonderful place to look for an unusual souvenir, such as a traditional khanjar *or dagger – still worn in some countries of the Arabian Gulf.*

Above: Camels were once the essential allies of the Bedu. They remain ubiquitous, many now being bred almost exclusively for racing and commanding very high prices. It's also possible to go on a leisurely camel ride, a surprisingly smooth experience in which the camel appears to be gliding over the sand.

Left: While the nomadic Bedu of yesteryear have settled for a sedentary life, the silence and beauty of the desert now draws the resident and visitor for day-long excursions in the dunes or for magical star-lit dinners.

Left: Falconry is the traditional sport of the Emirates, and it's possible to encounter the birds in town, since part of their training involves habituating them to noise and crowds.

Far left: The female falcon is larger than the male, probably to enable it to defend its brood. Being smaller, the males tend to be better hunters, flying at speeds of up to 100 kilometres an hour.

The sunny side of life

They say when a man is tired of London he's tired of life. The same is true of Dubai and the emirate has much to offer those prepared to look beyond the beaches, swimming pools and watering holes of luxury hotels – as enjoyable as these may be.

Sports comprise a major part of Dubai's leisure activities and there's an immense choice for spectators and participants alike, with splendid facilities. It's really no wonder the emirate has been called the 'Sporting Capital of the Middle East'.

A number of internationally renowned events are timed to coincide with the Dubai Shopping Festival in March (also the cooler part of the year), including the Dubai Tennis Championships, the Dubai Desert Classic (golf) and the world's richest horse-race, the Dubai World Cup.

November is another full sporting month and sees premier events such as the Dubai Rugby Sevens, the Emirates Grand Prix and the Dubai Duty Free Grand Prix (for powerboats, in which Dubai is a world leader), the UAE Marlboro Desert Challenge and the Dubai International Rally. Traditional sports such as dhow racing and camel races are held throughout winter.

For those who prefer to take part rather than watch, some options are golf, tennis, squash, jogging, cycling, horse-riding, ten-pin bowling, ice-skating, go-karting, flying, shooting and archery, while there are a number of well-equipped gyms in which to work out. Water sports are understandably popular and the warm water of the Gulf is ideal for swimming, boating, sailing, jet-skiing, game fishing and diving – the facilities, including some impressive marinas, are first class. For the younger set there are stomach-churning rides at water parks such as Wild Wadi and Wonderland.

Other enjoyable, healthy leisure activities include visits to Dubai's beaches or walking in one of the many parks or gardens, or alternatively along the Creek or corniche, quite a feature of the UAE.

Many of Dubai's residents have access to a 4x4 and drives into the desert, mountains or wadis, sometimes incorporating overnight camps, are popular. The arid landscape is extremely photogenic, particularly close to sunrise or sunset, and you're likely to see camels alongside the road while driving into the desert areas.

Visitors can enjoy a similar type of experience on a desert safari, which could include dune driving, camel riding, sand-skiing, falconry demonstrations and a trip to a Bedouin village, culminating with a traditional Arabian barbecue under the stars, complete with music, belly-dancing and hubble-bubble pipes.

Moving on to other activities, with an impressive duty-free shop at its modern airport and glitzy shopping malls, Dubai is an exciting place to shop, particularly at night when the malls can get quite crowded and the café society, sipping cappuccinos and espressos, watch the passing parade.

Visitors will enjoy Deira City Centre, where the biggest selection of shops is found; Wafi, arguably the most exclusive; and BurJuman, which slots in somewhere between the two. It seems as though nearly every jeweller, fashion house or perfume manufacturer is represented at one of these three centres, as well as specialists in Arabian goods such as musky perfumes, carpets, furniture, antiques and souvenirs.

Every March, Dubai holds its shopping festival, when special discounts, competitions and a vibrant carnival atmosphere enhance the shopping experience. During the quieter-but-hotter summer months, Dubai Summer Surprises takes place to attract visitors and shoppers to the emirate. This is a good time for bargain hunters, especially when the reduced travel and accommodation packages add to the value of it all.

But there are many alternatives to shopping. Since Dubai has aptly been described as 'the place where East meets West', it will come as no surprise that it's also a gourmet's delight, with a vast number of restaurants and cuisines – and prices to suit all pockets. There are also modern cinema complexes showing the latest hit films and, occasionally, shows by pop stars such as Bryan Adams, Sting and Westlife.

So much for the modern attractions, but what of the traditional side of Dubai?

The evocative souks, for example, are just as exciting as the upmarket shopping malls, particularly for those in search of spices, fabrics, gold jewellery and Persian carpets. Eating at an inexpensive Arabian pavement café could be just as memorable as an Italian meal at a five-star hotel, while searching out the areas where you can discover links with the halcyon days of dhow trading and pearl diving could be the highlight of your holiday.

Dubai has something for everyone: the choice is yours.

Previous spread: Emirates Golf Club was the first championship grass course in the Middle East. The spectacular clubhouse, designed in the style of a group of Bedouin tents, is one of the most recognised landmarks in international golf.

In Dubai, the fast pace of daily life in the city is tempered by serene moments, such as the sun setting over the Arabian Gulf, accompanied by the muezzin's calling the faithful to prayer.

Far left: Throughout Dubai, the urban landscape is interspersed with parks and gardens. Safa Park, with its attractive central pond and waterfall, is one of the most popular.

Left: Creek Park blends the attraction of its Creek-side location with large expanses of grass on which young and old alike can enjoy a wide variety of sports and games.

Below: Youngsters study one of the attractions on the southern bank of the Creek.

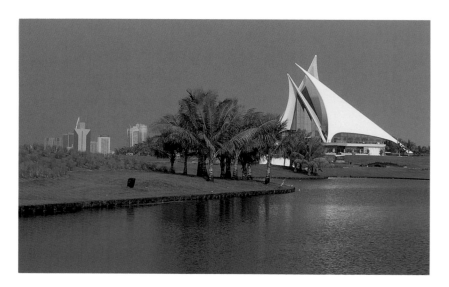

Top: The Dubai Creek Golf and Yacht Club is a 75-hectare oasis of greenery just minutes from the city centre.

Above: Besides an 18-hole, par 72 course, the Club boasts two spectacular club-houses, a marina, the region's first golfing academy, swimming pools and several fine restaurants and watering holes. Taking advantage of its location, it has also hosted some of Dubai's most memorable entertainment sessions.

Dubai has established itself as the sporting capital of the Gulf and hosts many world-class events that attract the biggest names in their games. Tiger Woods was the golfing star of the 2001 Desert Classic.

Left top and bottom: The Dubai Tennis Championship, owned and organised by Dubai Duty Free, is another world-class event that promotes Dubai to world television audiences and has, over the years, attracted some of the sport's major stars, such as Martina Hingis, Boris Becker, Jim Courier, Stefan Edberg and Goran Ivanisevic.

Right and below: Dubai is synonymous with the Dubai World Cup, the world's richest horse race, which every March attracts colourful crowds of up to 30,000 to Nad Al Sheba Racecourse. The race has been won by some of the world's greatest champion horses: Cigar, Singspiel, Silver Charm, Dubai Millennium and Captain Steve.

*In total contrast to the excitement and vibrancy
of the city, the stillness and beauty of the desert
can be experienced just a half-hour's drive away.
Desert safaris and dinners are a wonderful way
to explore another facet of Arabia.*

On the road to Hatta, an oasis a little more
than 100 kilometres from Dubai, you'll pass
majestic dunes of red sand before encountering
the stark but photogenic landscape of the Hajar
mountains. You may also experience a mirage.

The warm, clear waters of the Arabian Gulf are one of Dubai's prime attractions, ensuring its popularity as a holiday destination and a place to stay – particularly for those who enjoy sun and surf.

The rides and slides of Wild Wadi have become a 'must-do' on the itinerary of those seeking aquatic thrills – and spills.

Above: Even the architecture of some of Dubai's hotels reflects its seafaring heritage. The Jumeirah Beach Hotel, for one, has been innovatively designed to resemble a giant wave.

Left: Many of Dubai's superb resorts, such as the Ritz Carlton Hotel shown here, provide guests with direct access to the sea, as well as a wide choice of other facilities. Anyone for the beach? The pool? Water sports or tennis?

Right: The Royal Mirage Hotel, reminiscent in style of an Arabian fortress, offers luxurious interiors with a seductive Arabic ambience and beautifully landscaped grounds by the sea.

The Burj Al Arab's interior, reminiscent of The Thousand and One Nights, *offers a truly magical environment for guests and diners.*

The last word in luxury, the Burj Al Arab is an all-duplex-suites hotel which is rapidly becoming Dubai's most recognisable landmark. The hotel even purchased a fleet of eight Rolls Royce Silver Seraphs – the car manufacturer's largest single order – to take guests to and from the airport.

Besides its picturesque souks, Dubai has numerous shopping malls from which to choose; Deira City Centre, a destination in itself, is the largest and most-visited of them all. Promoting this shopping-paradise environment, the annual Dubai Shopping Festival in March attracts millions of visitors from all round the world.

Most of the globally recognised names in the fields of fashion, accessories, perfumes, electronics, furnishings and other consumer goods can be found in Dubai – and all at duty-free prices.

From a delicious Arabian lunch enjoyed by the beach, to a sumptuous evening buffet in a revolving restaurant or a tranquil meal in one of the city's many Japanese restaurants, the choice of culinary options is vast.

Some of the best entertainment acts in the world have been lured to perfom in Dubai.

The list of celebrities, such as Claudia Schiffer, who visit Dubai every year is a long one – and all of them become informal ambassadors for the city.

A futuristic outlook

*D*ubai has experienced phenomenal development in recent years. People who lived here more than 20 years ago would simply not recognise the city today. Along the eight-lane Sheikh Zayed highway for example (at the start of the main road from Dubai to Abu Dhabi), there are skyscrapers where there was previously nothing more than desert sand. Those who see this area from the sea nowadays refer to it as Dubai's 'Manhattan Skyline'.

Massive new projects are regularly announced, each one seemingly poised to eclipse previous – and even current – impressive developments.

In the world of commerce and industry, Dubai looks set to become a leader in technological development with the launch of Dubai Internet City, designed for today's 'borderless' world in which goods and services are traded around the clock. Companies such as software developers here enjoy a world-class infrastructure in a supportive environment, backed by the most streamlined company laws and labour regulations of any free zone in the world.

In a similar vein, the adjacent Dubai Media City is aiming to create a comprehensive media community, offering businesses a wealth of commercial benefits in a creative environment.

Realising the growing importance of tourism worldwide, the Dubai Crown Prince and UAE Minister of Defence, General Sheikh Mohammed bin Rashid Al Maktoum, recently predicted the emirate would have 50-million visitors a year by 2010 – five times the current figure. Despite the emirate's track record of setting seemingly unachievable targets, and hitting them, this astonished even the most seasoned observers.

Or did it? No sooner had Dubai International Airport's impressive new Sheikh Rashid Terminal opened, than details for a third, even larger terminal were announced. Designed for the exclusive use of the national carrier, Emirates, it will be equipped with 28 departure gates and some 64 parking bays and will assist Dubai in handling up to 60-million passengers a year by 2015. Collectively, the facilities for airlines and their passengers will be the most advanced available, designed to ensure Dubai remains at the cutting edge of civil aviation.

Emirates will also receive a significant boost when its growing fleet of modern aircraft takes delivery of the Airbus A380 double-decker jet, for which it's the launch customer. Even before then, Emirates will take delivery of the long-haul A340-500, capable of flying non–stop to New York, and will become the first regional operator to offer such a service.

To cater for the increase in tourism, a number of opulent new hotels have recently opened in Dubai while many others – including more affordable ones – are planned. A problem that may have hindered hotel and resort development in the past is the limited availability of beach properties, but even this has now been addressed – and in the most dynamic of ways.

A massive development, Palm Islands is set to add 120 kilometres of beachfront to the Dubai coastline. The project consists of two identical man-made, palm-shaped islands, *each* incorporating up to 40 boutique hotels, 2,000 residential villas, two marinas (with a combined berthing capacity for 300 yachts and 100 mega-yachts), shopping complexes and cinemas. The 'trunk' of the first island also includes the Middle East's first marine park.

Dubai Marina is another of the city's bold developments (and the first where foreigners will be able to buy property). Inspired by waterfront developments overseas, Dubai Marina will be built in phases during the next 10 to 15 years. The 3.5-kilometre waterway running parallel to Jumeirah Beach will provide 10,000 people with desirable waterfront living. More than just an upper-class neighbourhood, it will also feature cafés, restaurants and shops as well as world-class golf courses and a string of beachside resorts.

The developers are also involved in other exciting residential estates, one being Emirates Hills, part of a 20-kilometre project set around three golf courses, offering a secure family lifestyle in a parkland environment.

Just about everywhere in Dubai, shopping centres are being constructed or enlarged, while new apartment blocks reach for the skies. But even these haven't impacted on another massive development, Dubai Festival City, scheduled to open in 2004. This complex, which will be built along a prime four-kilometre stretch of Dubai's Creek, will feature a 55-storey tower, an 8,000-capacity amphitheatre, 80 restaurants, shops, hotels, cinemas, offices and apartments.

With the foresight of Dubai's ruling Maktoum family, and so many developments on the go, the future of this progressive emirate looks very bright indeed.

Previous spread: The development of Sheikh Zayed Road as a business centre has attracted many business hotels. The most spectacular is that in the Emirates Towers complex which, seen from afar, towers over the rest of the area's buildings.

The Dubai World Trade Centre, seen here between the minarets of a nearby mosque, is one of Dubai's landmarks. The view from the top of the tower, especially at dusk when the city lights are turned on, is dazzling.

Colourful balloon sculptures mark the launch of Dubai Festival City while across the Creek Emirates Towers forms a striking backdrop.

The office, hotel and apartment towers of vertiginous heights which line both sides of busy Sheikh Zayed Road are evidence of the number of multi-national companies which have established their headquarters in the fast-growing city.

Far left: The Emirates Towers complex comprises a 400-room luxury hotel with eight restaurants, an office tower and a shopping boulevard. The office building, rising to 350 metres, is presently the tallest building in the Middle East and Europe.

Left: Even by Dubai standards, the dazzling Dusit Dubai is an impressive structure and underlines the keen interest shown by major international hotel groups to invest in the emirate.

75

Dubai Media City, the neighbour of Dubai Internet City, is wired with the latest telecommunication and transmission technology to provide regional as well as global media with an environment from which to produce, publish and broadcast.

Dubai Internet City, opened in October 2000, sprang from the desert in exactly one year. Its buildings and surrounding landscaped areas reflect the region's traditional heritage, while meeting the needs of the contemporary office worker.

By facilitating the convergence of members of the IT and media industry in a purpose-built location, the Dubai Technology, E-commerce and Media Free-Zone Authority is also making possible frequent face-to-face meetings – which still remains one of the most effective ways of doing business!

In Dubai you're never too far from a cybercafé and, once there, from friendly staff help.

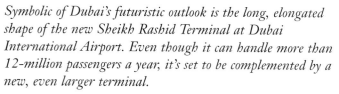

Symbolic of Dubai's futuristic outlook is the long, elongated shape of the new Sheikh Rashid Terminal at Dubai International Airport. Even though it can handle more than 12-million passengers a year, it's set to be complemented by a new, even larger terminal.

Above and right: Dubai Duty Free, one of the most successful in the world, offers a massive range of 65,000 products. Among its main attractions are its promotions; the 'Finest Surprise' where the winner drives away in a luxury car, and the 'Millenium Millionaire', where the prize is $1 million.

Photographic Credits

Al-Futtaim Investments   73T

Connection Sports
Management (CSM)   67L, 67R

Dubai Civil Aviation   78L, 78R, 79

Dubai Duty Free   54T, 54B (L& R)

Dusit Dubai   75

Emirates Golf Club   44/45,

Motivate Publishing   21T, 39B,

Shankar Adiseshan: 2, 4/5, 8/9, 14T, 14B, 15, 17, 18T, 18B, 19,
                          20, 21B, 22, 23, 24/25, 28T, 29T, 29B, 30,
                          31, 34, 35T, 35B, 36, 37T, 39T, 43, 48/49,
                          50, 51T, 51B, 52T, 55, 56, 57, 60T, 64, 65,
                          73B, 76L, 76R, 77T, 77B

Ferrari, Jorge   12/13, 40, 52B

Jebreili, Kamran   16, 28B, 60B

Jumeirah International   58, 62, 63, 68/69, 74, 75

Khan, Irfan   72

Milne Home, Bob   Cover, 1, 41

Royal Mirage   61, 66

Shah, Aziz   53

Zandi, Dariush   32, 33, 37B, 38, 42

T: top, B: bottom, L: left, R: right

- Published with the support
  and encouragement of